Planning a Garden

*A Canadian guide to successful vegetable
and flower gardening*
GASTON CHARBONNEAU

Greey de Pencier Publications 1975

ISBN 0-919872-09-3

Cover photograph by Malak
Drawings by Pierre Bachand
Design and art direction by Ron Butler
Translation by Jean Hamilton Baudouin
Publishing consultants: Editek

The assistance of the Directors of
Montreal's Botanical Garden are gratefully
acknowledged.

To my son Sylvain

Contents

The Kitchen garden 13
Artichoke 19
Asparagus *(Asparagus officinalis)*.. 20

Basil 21
Beans 22
Beets *(Beta vulgaris)* 23
Broccoli *(Brassica oleracea)* 24
Brussels sprouts 25

Cabbage 26
Cantaloupe melon 27
Carrots *(Daucus carota)* 28
Cauliflower 29
Celery *(Apium graveolens)* 30
Chervil 31
Chicory 32
Chinese cabbage .... • 33
Chives 34
Cress 35
Cucumber 36

Dill 37

Egg-plant *(Solanum melangena)* 38
Endive 39
Endive, broad-leaved 40

Fennel 41

Garlic 42
Gourd 43

Indian corn (sweet corn) 44

Laurel 45
Leek 46
Lettuce 47

Mushroom 48

Onion 49

Contents (continued)

Parsley 50
Parsnip 51
Pimento, mild and strong 52
Potato 53
Pumpkin 54

Radish 55

Savory 65
Spinach 66
Spring Onion 67

Tomato 68
Turnip (rutabaga) 70

Watermelon 71

Herbs for seasoning 72

Annual flowers 73
Ageratum 77
Alyssum 78
Amaranth 79

Bellflower *(Campanula)* 80

Calendula 81
Carnation 82
Celosia *(Cockscomb)* 83
Centaurea *(Bachelor's button)* 84
China-aster 85
Cineraria 86
Cosmos 87

Dahlia 88

Gilliflower 89

Everlasting (Honesty) *(Lunaria annua)* 90

Morning glory (Bindweed) *(Convolvulus)* ... 91

Nasturtium 92

Petunia *(Saint Joseph)* 93

Contents (continued)

Snapdragon 94
Sweet pea 95

Perennial plants 97
Chrysanthemum 101

Geranium 102

Larkspur 103

Pansy 104
Peony 105

Windows, Balcony gardens 107

Seed Calendar for Garden Flowers 113

Vegetable Seed Calendar for Kitchen Gardens 114
Vegetable Seed Calendar for Kitchen Gardens 115

Annual Calendar 116

Maintenance 119

Preface

We live in a complex and difficult time — a time of global crises, faltering economies, and shortages of such basic human requirements as energy and food. The pace of life has become increasingly hectic and, as it has done so, many of us have begun our own personal searches for at least some token return to a simpler, more tranquil way of living.

As the pressures of life in the industrialized Western world have increased, great numbers of people have found relief in a renewal of interest in gardening. There is a special pride one feels as a plant — almost any plant — springs from the earth and grows into something beautiful in response to the patient care it has received from the person who has grown it.

If this book is your first introduction to gardening, prepare yourself for a new and exciting experience. If you have worked with plants before and have just now decided to try your hand at a kitchen garden, then your satisfaction will be increased every time you sit down to a meal that includes something fresh from your garden, something that cost you nothing but a few cents and many pleasant hours outdoors.

Whether your aim is to supplement the family diet, to beautify your back lot, or simply to add living colour to the inside of a room, you will find the practical advice you need between the covers of this little book.

Gaston Charbonneau

The kitchen garden

When you decide to begin your vegetable gardening, you and your family will have the opportunity to observe the different steps of vegetable growing. Be sure to select the varieties that your family would like to have for food. Remember, it is *not* imperative to know everything about plants. The main point is to be ready to work and to have the desire to succeed.

Preparation

Plants need some attention in order to germinate and grow, and they require proper soil. In choosing the site for your garden, it is advisable to find a well-drained and sunny spot, properly sheltered from extremes in the weather. The north or northeast side of a building as well as tree shade should be avoided. When the best location has been chosen, a plan should be drawn. If you wish, frame the garden with posts and vertical boards; this makes it easy to maintain and it looks neat. Your scale drawing must show exact dimensions, so that you can work out the number of rows and the planting lay-out. Notes should be taken of any information relating to your garden.

Soil: In certain areas, the soil is just not good enough to support vigorous growth. Should this be the case for the garden site you have chosen, you will have no alternative but to set your boards in place, dig down about 10 in. (25 cm), remove all of the old soil you have thus turned, and replace it with good, balanced top soil.

The most prudent course to follow is either to purchase an inexpensive soil-testing kit — which comes with complete instructions and is itself an invaluable source of instruction for the new amateur gardener — or to send off a sample of your soil to the Department of Agriculture for analysis. Armed with the specific information, you should then consult your nursery. They should be able to tell you whether or not your soil is adequate, and what to do if it isn't.

Doing this preliminary work in the fall will save you time in the spring, when the soil should be prepared for planting. Dig to a depth of 7 or 8 in. (18-20 cm) turning the soil over as you work. Before seeding, break up and rake the surface carefully to remove stones and make the surface level.

Fertilizer: Most plants — and this includes vegetables — respond well to a proper application of fertilizer to the soil. Select a well-balanced chemical fertilizer and follow the manufacturer's directions as closely as possible whether you are planting seeds or developing seedlings that you have started indoors earlier in the spring. There are two cardinal rules to follow when spreading fertilizer: first, *never* sprinkle fertilizer on any part of a growing seedling or small plant; second, don't use too much fertilizer. If you do, you will kill or seriously injure the plant. Even slight overdoses to some crops will produce great masses of foliage, thick stems — and almost no vegetables.

After your plants are properly placed, a small quantity of fertilizer should be spread around the plant from 4 to 6 in. (10 to 15 cm) from the stem and mixed in with a rake. For seeds, fertilizer is sprinkled on each side of the row and about 6 in. (15 cm) from the seeds. This latter operation can wait for germination time. A light scattering at two or three week intervals should suffice. Passages or walks around the garden should be kept to a minimum, since the bare soil promotes evaporation. If there is not enough moisture, growth will be impaired.

When to sow

Generally, sowing or planting should not begin until the danger of late frost is over. As a rule, there is no problem after the full moon in May. Maturing time must also be taken into account for each vegetable. In a case when three of four months are required, seeding should be very early or the plants should be started indoors.

Sowing seeds

When the soil has been fully prepared and watered, straight rows should be marked with tight cord. Adequate depth is necessary so be sure to check each seed packet for instructions. For very small seeds, we suggest that you mix them with flour so that they may be traced easily and planted in a white line at the bottom of the row. Then, using your hands or a rake, push the soil onto the seeds and apply enough light pressure to the soil to make it firm. When the plants start growing, thin out the least vigorous and leave enough space for the remaining plants to grow. Large-size seeds should be buried in small holes and carefully covered with soil. Each row should be labelled. Constant moisture must be maintained with light sprinkling. Remember that crowding does not promote good crops.

Indoor seeding and transplanting

For an early start, sowing is best done indoors in pots or flats. A sterilized mixture of leaf mould and "potting soil" may be used as the potting medium. Take a large container of the mixture and drench it with water for the night. Next day drain off excess water and fill each pot or each flat with the planting mixture to three-quarters capacity. The mixture should not be compressed. Proceed with seeding about $1/8$ in. (.50 cm apart) and cover the seeds with a thin layer of the medium. If the seeds are fine just press them gently into the soil. Then, place the flats or pots in pans of water for base watering. During germination, cover pots with clear plastic sheet to retain moisture. Choose a semi-shaded spot. When the young shoots emerge, a great deal of light is required. Remove the plastic and put the pots in a bright window. But make sure plants do not get too much heat or they will become soft and "leggy". If your plants are in flats, carefully prick out the best young seedlings when they are about $1^1/2$ in. (4 cm) and move them to other boxes or pots. If your plants are in pots, a week before transplanting outside, select the best plants and destroy the others by cutting at soil levels. Then put your seedlings outside for a few days to harden them up (or get them used to outside temperatures). When transplanting outdoors, press the young plants into the soil just above the roots. This operation should be performed at dusk or on a dark day. Water heavily, but carefully as not to damage the plants.

Watering

Water is a "must" for plant life. Before watering, however, soil requirements and drainage must be checked. Excess water encourages disease and insects, while drought will affect vegetable quality. Watering should not be delayed until the leaves are shrivelled or the soil becomes hard and cracked. For perfect watering, roots should be kept moist. If they are, this will carry the plants for a few days, even in dry weather. Unless sufficient water is given, the soil will harden and rooting will only take place near the surface.

Plant maintenance

Weeding and hoeing are other important aspects of vegetable growing. The goal of weeding is to destroy unwanted growth thus conserving soil water and fertilizers. Moreover, some weeds contribute to insect proliferation. Unfortunately, hoeing results in breaking up the surface of the soil thus increasing evaporation. Even so, this operation is complementary to weeding and is most important in early spring to increase heat penetration. To avoid root damage, hoeing should not go too deep or too close. In some cases, earthing up will also be needed bring soil around the plant base. This stimulates good rooting. These tasks must be carried out as often as required, but always before watering. Insects should also be checked and it is wise to use preventive insecticides. Should the presence of insects be noted, they must be destroyed immediately. The insecticide to be used should be selected by an experienced gardener or by your nursery.

Rotation

The drawing of your garden made earlier is most important because it will then be possible to rotate the placing of your vegetable plants the following year. To avoid soil exhaustion, it is advisable to change your garden's location every few years. For a good crop, remember that fertilizing is beneficial. Make notes of your garden's yield. It will then be easy for you to compare different varieties of a given vegetable and to pick the one you like best.

Artichoke

This vegetable, little known in Canada a few years ago, is fast gaining in popularity. It is considered a luxury and is in great demand. It grows to a height of 3 to 3 1/2 ft. (90 to 100 cm) and its straight stem holds a rosette of large leaves, whitish green on the underside and cotton-like on the upper side.

Because of our climate, the artichoke is not a perennial in Canada. Seed-beds must be prepared in February or March or, new plants can be propagated from suckers.

Young plants are pot-grown in preparation for outdoor planting, which is done early in June. The tops of the plant will have thick, fleshy scales by the end of the fall. Cut artichoke tops for use before the centre scales separate and when they can still be broken off easily when bent away from the plant.

A very rich soil is required and it must be kept moist. Spacing should be about 12 in. (30 cm) and plants should be earthed up regularly.

Asparagus

Asparagus officinalis

It is advisable to buy year-old asparagus plants from your dealer. Alternatively, you may use seeds that have been soaked in water 80° F (240° C) for two or three days. Plant the seeds about two in. (5 cm) apart and cover them with an inch of soil. Germination occurs after two or three weeks. In the spring, thin the plants further, so that they are 18 in. (45 cm) apart and in rows 4 ft. (120 cm) apart. The furrows should be about 12 in. (30 cm) deep. Don't begin to cut stems until the third year. In that year cutting should be limited to a period of two weeks and only the stronger stems should be cut. Cutting time may be increased by a week in subsequent years. Cutting should be stopped by the end of July when the plant begins to prepare for the winter. For harvestings, use a sharp knife and insert it about 1 in. (2.5 cm) below the surface of the ground. To be ready for cutting, stems should be ³/₈ in. (1 cm) in diameter, 5.5 in. (14 cm) long, and 85 per cent green.

Earthing up should be done regularly.

Basil

Besides being a seasoning plant, basil is ornamental and is easily grown in a pot.

Two seed-beds should be made, the first one indoors by early April and the second in the ground by May 20.

Spacing between rows should be 20 in. (50 cm) and between plants 5 to 6 in. (13 to 15 cm).

A light, rich soil is necessary. Weeding and hoeing should be done regularly. Constant moisture should be maintained.

When basil is grown for seasoning, the varieties commonly used are Great Green and Lettuce Laurel Green.

After May 15, basil plants may be purchased in shopping centres and nurseries. All you have to do is put them in the ground.

Beans

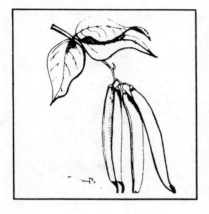

This plant, of American origin, is very important to our diet because of the high nutritive value of the seed.

It is quite easy to grow. Planting must be done in a good gardening soil, well fertilized, with good drainage and in a sunny place. Late spring frosts can be fatal to the crop. Seeding is best done early in June, in rows, about 2 in. (5 cm) deep. Spacing for rows must be 20 to 24 in. (50 to 60 cm) and for plants from 2 to 3 in. (5 to 7.5 cm).

To increase production, pick the pods as fast as they appear.

By seeding regularly, you can harvest continuously throughout the whole season. As a precaution against mildew, never walk between rows when the plants are wet. It takes 52 to 70 days for the plants to mature fully.

Beets

Beta vulgaris

This annual yields a good crop when it is planted in the right sort of soil. It is easy to grow, and the beet roots are especially delicious when they have attained half their full size. Sowing should be ½ in. (about 1 cm) deep, as soon as the spring soil is ready. Full growth takes 55 to 70 days.

Spacing between rows should be 12 to 18 in. (30 to 45 cm) and between plants 2 in. (5 cm). If your main sowing is done by June 15, you'll have a crop in time for fall pickling. You can keep beets in a cool place for use during the winter.

Fresh manure should never be used; weeding and hoeing must be done often. Many different varieties of this popular food plant are available. The early varieties, which are sometimes zoned for indoors only, have a tender foliage that can be served in the same way as spinach.

Broccoli

Brassica oleracea

Broccoli belongs to the cauliflower family and it requires the same sort of attention. It is fast-growing, so indoor planting should be done in March.

Seed-beds should be ¼ in. (5 mm) deep and outdoor planting ought to be done by the end of May. Spacing between plants should be 15 to 24 in. (37 to 61 cm) and between rows about 3 ft. (90 cm), depending on the variety.

This is a fine vegetable and a good producer throughout the whole season. Picking must be done before the flowers open, that is, before they turn mustard-yellow. From seeding time to full growth takes 60 to 70 days.

The most popular varieties are Early Propageno and Hybrid Cleopatra.

Brussels sprouts

Brussels sprouts are not widely grown in Canada. Nevertheless, they are quite easy to grow and require about the same care as cabbage.

Indoor sowing should be done between April 15 and 20. Outdoor transplanting may be done early in June. Spacing should be 32 in. (80 cm) between rows and 20 in. (50 cm) between plants. The soil should be worked regularly by hoeing and weeding. Fertilizers should be applied regularly. Early in September, the terminal shoots should be pinched and this will help to form uniform and firm buds. Harvesting begins at the end of August and may last until early December.

This kind of cabbage is distinguished by its loose head and by the small mottled buds (sprouts) that grow along the stem. These small buds are the edible parts. On the average, brussels sprouts need 90 to 95 days to reach full maturity.

Cabbage

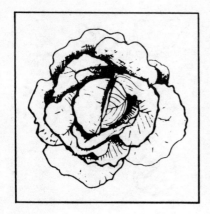

Cabbage is an ancient vegetable. There are now many improved varieties.

Three crops are possible. First seeding should be indoors, between March 15 and 20, in ¼ in. (5 mm) furrows. Replanting should be done every 2 in. (5 cm). Final planting should be done early in May. Spacing should be about 2 ft. (60 cm) between rows and 18 in. (46 cm) between plants.

For the second crop make a seedbed about a month after the first planting. To be on the safe side, it is preferable to make this seed-bed indoors. Indoor replanting will not be necessary this time: plant straight into the ground. Finally, for the fall harvest, seeding should be done by early June, and it may be done directly into the ground.

Cabbage is greedy, so you must give it a very rich and well-drained soil. Never plant in the same plot for two consecutive years. Roots should be dug up and burned in the fall.

Cantaloupe melon

For an early crop, sow seeds indoors in March or April. When the plants are 1 or 2 in. (2.5 or 5 cm) high, transplant in pots so as to avoid root damage when the time arrives to transplant into the ground.

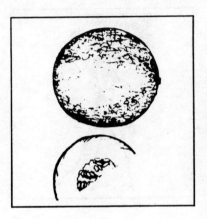

If you decide on outdoor planting in the ground, wait until early June, because melons dislike the cold. Mounds containing six or eight seeds should be built 4 to 5 ft. (1.25 to 1.5 m) apart. When the young plants come up, choose three strong ones and remove all the others. The soil must be very rich. For the best flavour, melons should be picked when they have reached maturity, that is when the fruit comes off easily. Pruning will result in better fruit. If the main stem has four or five leaves, all but two of them should be cut off. Side branches should be cut off above the fourth leaf. Topping should only be done on plants during the growing period and only in warm weather.

Carrots

Daucus carota

The carrot is a most popular vegetable in Canada and has a high nutritive value. It is easy to grow and sowing can be done early in the spring, as soon as the soil is ready. So as to have fresh, young carrots throughout the season, do some planting every 15 days. Note that seeding done around June 25 will give you a fall crop, i.e. winter supplies.

Carrot growing should be done in a light and well fertilized soil. Between 65 and 80 days are required for full maturity. Seeds are planted ½ in. (1 cm) deep. Spacing between rows should be about 12 in. (30 cm) and between plants from 1 to 2 in. (approximately 3 to 5 cm). Fly grubs must be fought vigorously; your nursery will supply a suitable insecticide.

Cauliflower

Cauliflower is one of the most widely grown vegetables in Canada. With proper attention it can yield two main crops, an early one and another in the fall.

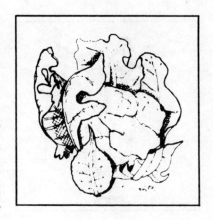

For the early crop, seeds should be planted indoors in March, in rows 1/4 in. (.5 cm) deep. Pot or box replanting is done when the young plants are about 3 in. (about 8 cm) high. Early in May, transplant into the ground with 24 in. (60 cm) between rows and 18 in. (45 cm) between plants. The heads should be tied up when they have reached the size of cups, to protect them and help them whiten.

For the main crop, sowing should be done early in May, followed by outdoor transplanting early in July. Row spacing is 28 in. (70 cm) and plant spacing 20 in. (50 cm).

A slightly clayish and well-fertilized soil is necessary for cauliflower. Water with fertilizers once during growth. Good drainage is essential. Between 50 to 65 days are required for full growth.

Celery

Apium graveolens

The ancient Greeks and Romans considered celery a medicinal plant and today it is regarded as a crisp and tender nutritional one with a taste reminiscent of almonds. It should be planted indoors by early March and should be barely covered with earth. Germination is slow and takes from 15 to 25 days, depending on the temperature and the humidity. As soon as the little plants are 1 or 1½ in. (about 3 to 4 cm) high, they should be replanted in flats with 2 in. (5 cm) spacing. In May they should be planted out of doors in rows with 9 to 10 in. (23 to 25 cm) spacing. Boxes may be used, or small pots with one plant in each.

When outdoor planting is done at the end of May or early in June, spacing between rows should be 2 ft. (60 cm). A very rich black soil and high moisture are required. Watering with fertilizers may be done during growth. To reach maturity the plants need 95 to 105 days. Earthing up should be done every 15 days.

Chervil

This plant came originally from southeast Russia. It does not grow much over 12 in. (30 cm) high. A moisture-retaining soil must be used. Grow in a semi-shaded place and remember that frequent watering is necessary. During excessively warm periods, the only vegetation is a premature flowering.

Spring or fall growing is advisable, with seeding in May or August. Rows should be 15 to 18 in. (38 to 46 cm) apart. Seeds should be planted in a compact soil, with very light covering.

Chervil should be picked six weeks after planting. Cutting must be done at ground level. Leaves are yellow, tender, and scented.

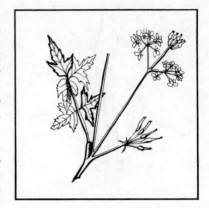

Chicory

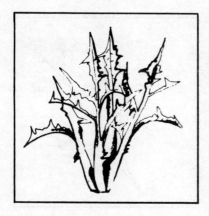

Chicory is easy to grow and is used mainly in salads. The taste is somewhat reminiscent of asparagus or dandelion.

Seed-beds should be made as soon as the soil is warm. Furrows should be ¼ in. (5 mm) deep. For the main harvest, seeds are planted by the end of June or early in July. Spacing between rows should be 18 in. (46 cm) and for plants 10 to 12 in. (25 to 30 cm). To maintain this spacing, rows will have to be thinned out when young shoots appear after germination. Surplus plants may be transplanted to extend the rows.

Your crop will be good if the soil is very rich or regularly fertilized. Full maturity requires about 95 days.

Chinese cabbage

Chinese cabbage is a rather new vegetable to Canada, but it is easy to grow and yields a good crop. Growth is rapid and an early crop is possible in addition to the regular one. For an early crop, indoor planting should be done in April and garden transplanting early in the spring. As for the regular crop, seeds should be planted in the ground at the end of June or early in July.

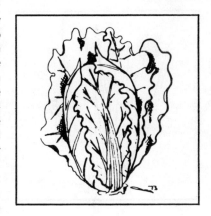

Spacing between rows must be 2 ft. (60 cm) and between plants 10 in. (25 cm). Harvesting may start two months later and continue to the end of October. Handle this vegetable carefully, because the foliage is soft and is easily damaged. Storage for many months is possible in a cellar. This plant does not need the same amount of fertilizing as cauliflower, but high humidity is required for a good crop.

Chives

This perennial plant comes from Europe. Chives is well known as a seasoning vegetable, and it thrives in almost any soil.

For fast growth and to obtain plants with tender, tasty stems, use a rich soil. In the winter, the plants may be kept in pots.

Propagation is generally done by the division of root tufts, although seed-beds may be made in April or May. Cutting should be done monthly since this will make the stems sprout again, more vigorously, and the chives will be fresher.

You will be able to keep your chives planted in the same place for years, since it is a perennial. To protect the plant against the cold, especially in winter, cover the roots with leaves or mulch. In the spring, do a clean-up and you'll have a fine supply of chives for another year.

Cress

This plant grows mainly beside brooks and streams. Although its natural setting is beside running water, cress may also be grown in kitchen gardens. Dig a trench 10 or 12 in. (25 to 30 cm) deep and 24 to 30 in. (60 to 75 cm) wide. In the trench put four to five in. (10 to 12.5 cm) of good soil. Seeds should not be covered but soil should be pressed in firmly, and watered frequently. Two to three rows may be planted in each trench and the cress will be ready to harvest in six or eight weeks.

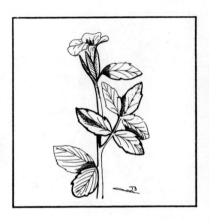

Propagation can be done with seeds or with leaf cuttings placed in water. When you are collecting cress, cut the stems about 5 in. (12 cm) from the terminal buds. Refrigeration is necessary and the foliage should be kept moist until it is served.

Cucumber

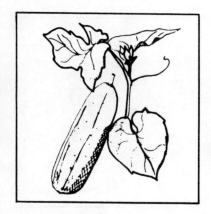

This is a very popular vegetable. It appears often on the table, either in salads or pickled in the form of gherkins or slices. Because of its high water content, it is considered rather low in nutritive value.

For some years, cucumbers have been affected by diseases that are almost impossible to check. We would advise you to consult your government agricultural representative or nursery for instructions on dealing with those diseases.

Seeding is done on hillocks 5 ft. (1.5 m) apart, early in June. After germination has taken place, only three or four plants should be retained on each hillock. Cucumbers should be picked while still young. They dislike the cold and manage with a moderate amount of moisture.

Dill

Dill grows wild in Europe.

Seeds are gathered in September and they are oval in shape and flat. They are commonly used as spicing for pickles and canned foods. Seeding must be done in May or June.

Spacing for rows should be 24 in. (about 60 cm) and for plants 3 to 4 in. (8 to 10 cm). When the plants are 1 or 2 in. (3 to 5 cm) high, thin them out to the required spacing.

Hoeing and weeding must be done frequently, especially after heavy rain.

The seeds should be picked in September or October.

Egg-plant

Solanum melangena

This plant from India thrives in a warm climate.

For a good crop, indoor sowing must be done in February or March. Growing procedure is about the same as for the tomato. The egg-plant should be transplanted into a rich soil at the end of June.

Spacing should be 2 to 3 feet (60 to 90 cm) between plants and between rows.

Pick when the fruit has reached good size and the skin is glossy.

Great care must be taken to protect the plant from its worst enemy, the flying insect Coccinella. This insect should be dealt with as soon as it appears, or your crop will be in serious danger. Consult your nursery about what to do.

The egg-plant is very sensitive to frost, and it needs constant moisture. You are more likely to succeed if you use a rich soil that will retain moisture well. Two varieties of the plant are popular with gardeners: American Beauty and Improved New York.

Endive

Endive is beginning to appear on Canadian tables. It is being served cooked, in salads, or with bread-crumbs.

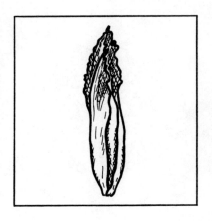

The seeds are planted quite deep, in a good warm soil. Spacing between rows must be 18 to 20 in. (45 to 50 cm) and between plants 5 to 6 in. (13 to 15 cm). The leaves are harvested at the end of October or early November. The roots are then dug up; small and medium-sized roots are kept and the large ones are thrown away. They should be allowed to dry for a few days, but out of the sun. Root-ends should all be cut to the same length.

For forcing, roots are kept in a cool basement at 50° to 60° F (10° to 12° C). They are arranged side by side and separated by a little soil; then they are covered with 7 to 8 in. (18 to 20 cm) of light black soil. After 20 to 25 days, each endive plant should have a nice top and this should be cut off with some of the root. The roots produced by the forcing are useless and should not be kept.

If you do not want to force the roots, store them in a cold cellar at 30° to 40° F (0° to 5° C) for the winter.

Endive, broad-leaved

This endive's leaves are broad and rippled or rolled, with notches on the edges. It is a plant that thrives in cold fall weather. It is easily grown and it gives a good crop.

Seeding is done early in the spring, as soon as the soil has warmed up. Spacing for rows must be 18 to 24 in. (45 to 60 cm) and for plants 12 in. (30 cm).

When the plants are two-thirds grown, earthing up should be done to ensure good whitening. The crop will be ready by the end of June or early in July. If you are looking for a fall crop, do your sowing late in June or during the first few days of July. When it has been picked, the crop should be whitened, or placed in the dark to make the foliage yellow before eating.

The plant's rosette may also be tied up during growth to encourage whitening or yellowing, and this will improve the flavour and the tenderness. From 85 to 90 days are required for full maturity.

Fennel

This plant is of Mediterranean origin. It is grown here as an annual. It reaches a height of about 3.5 ft. (about 1 m). The stem is rather thick. The plant blossoms in August and reaches full maturity in September.

A well-drained and fertile plot is required. Its roots enable fennel to survive drought fairly well.

Sowing must be done early in May. Rows should be placed 24 to 30 in. (60 to 75 cm), and plants 5 to 6 in. (12.5 to 15 cm) apart. Frequent and heavy watering is necessary right up to the time of picking. Preferably, the entire plant should be picked when flowering begins. Fennel stands up well to early frost.

Garlic

This plant comes from Central Asia and flowering occurs only very rarely. Bulbs are obtained by planting offshoots in the month of May. Only offshoots of a really good size should be used, otherwise the result will be puny and pathetic plants. Leave a space of 18 inches (46 cm) between rows and 4 inches (10 cm) between plants. Deep planting is never successful, so offshoot tips should be barely covered with soil. The bulb will form just below the surface of the ground. Be careful not to push it down, when hoeing or weeding.

For successful growing the most important points are: fertilize; make sure the soil is well drained; plant early; and take good care of your plants by weeding and hoeing regularly.

Before picking, wait until the stems have withered and turned yellow. Braid the bulbs into ropes and hang in a well-ventilated place.

Gourd

Growing procedure is exactly the same as for the pumpkin. According to the variety, seeding should be done, as soon as the soil has warmed up, on hillocks 4 to 10 ft. (1.20 to 3 m) apart. Summer gourds can be brought in only after attaining their full size, but they are much sweeter and more tender when they are 4 to 5 in. (10 to 12.5 cm) high than they are at crop time.

The mounds should be well fertilized, and thinned after germination to leave only three plants on each mound.

The summer gourd is often called the marrow.

The winter gourd is picked in October and is easy to keep. The summer gourd takes about 52 days to reach maturity, whereas 110 days or so are required for the winter gourd to mature.

Indian corn (sweet corn)

Corn thrives in any kind of garden soil, as long as the drainage is good and proper mounds are made. Outdoor sowing should be done at the end of May in furrows about 1 in. (2.5 cm) deep. Planting should be done with the spacing of 12 in. (30 cm) between plants in all directions. Use more seeds than necessary and thin out after growing starts. A very thin covering of soil is recommended. Then, after germination, earth the plants up gradually, a bit at a time. Sowing should never be done in a single row, which would give small, misshapen cobs. We suggest that you plant several varieties, so that you can harvest several times during the season. Corn takes 70 to 100 days to reach full maturity.

Of the many varieties, here are four that cover the whole season: very early: Golden Mine (52 days); early: Golden Bantam King-Cross (62 days); late: Butter and Sugar (70 days); very late: Hybrid Golden Bantam (84 days).

Laurel

From southern Europe, this plant must be kept inside during the winter. Laurel symbolizes glory, victory and peace. Its fruit-covered stems have long been used to crown successful university students, whence the word "baccalaureate".

Laurel is nearly always grown in pots — small ones — for best results. A firm soil is recommended, with good drainage. Well-diluted liquid fertilizer should be used once or twice a month.

During the winter, reduce the watering, stop fertilizing completely, and keep the plant in a cool place (55° to 60° F) (13° to 16° C)

Take precautions against draughts, or your laurel plant will not bloom.

Leek

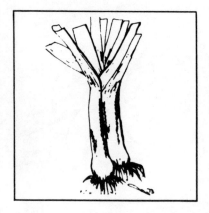

Belonging to the onion family, the leek has a special flavour, sweeter than the onion. In March, indoor sowing may be done in rows ¹/₄ in. (5 mm) deep. Outdoor planting is done at the end of May. Spacing between rows should be 24 in. (60 cm) and between plants 4 to 6 in. (10 to 15 cm).

To get strong plants, cut off about one-third of the stem when replanting. For the main crop, seeds are planted early in May, with row spacing of 24 in. (60 cm). Later on, thin plants to 4 or 6 in. (10 to 15 cm). Leeks need much fertilizing, as well as hoeing and weeding. Moderate earthing-up around the plant increases the whitening. Harvesting begins in September and lasts until December.

For full maturity, 100 to 125 days are required.

Lettuce

Many varieties of lettuce are available, but the chief ones are leaf lettuce and cabbage lettuce.

For early crops sow indoors in rows ¹/₄ in. (.5 cm) deep, in March or April. Temperature must be kept below 75° F (22° C); otherwise the seeds will not come up. Lettuce plants are cold-resistant, so planting may be done as soon as it is possible to work the ground.

Rows of leaf lettuce should be 15 to 18 in. (38 to 45 cm) apart, and rows of cabbage lettuce at least 10 in. (25 cm) apart. For leaf lettuce, a space of 6 to 8 in. (15 to 20 cm) is big enough between plants. Pick only the outside leaves, and you will have fresh lettuce until the end of July. Hoe your lettuce often, but not too deeply. Weed often as well. Between 50 and 75 days are required for full growth.

Lettuce does not like high temperatures, so its best seasons are spring and fall.

Mushroom

Successful mushroom growing depends on a combination of scientific and empirical knowledge.

To get good crops requires years of experience, as well as ideal growing conditions of a sort that the beginner cannot easily create.

I will add simply that mushrooms are grown in a bed of manure that has been allowed to stand for 16 to 20 days and whose temperature is 90° F (32° C). This means that the storage room must be kept at an average temperature of 130° F (55° C) for several days. Moreover, mushrooms are very sensitive to diseases and to insects; consequently, they need a great deal of care and attention.

For these reasons, I advise amateurs against attempting to grow mushrooms.

Onion

Onions require well-drained soil very rich in leaf mould, and regular weeding. For spring crops, early March sowing is necessary. Since the cold presents no problems, early May sowing may be done in the ground. For indoor sowing, the spacing between rows should be 3 in. (8 cm). About a month after sowing, cut off the plants' tips to promote stronger rooting and faster growth. Plants should be thinned out to $1/2$ to 1 in. (1 to 2 cm) and placed in an airy sunny spot. Transplant into the ground as early as possible in May. Spacing between rows should be 15 to 18 in. (38 to 45 cm) and between plants 2 in. (5 cm).

The onions are ripe when the stems fall over or collapse. After this happens, wait for 10 days before picking to give the onions time to dry out and reach perfect maturity.

Parsley

Parsley is of ancient Mediterranean origin. It is an annual plant and is easy to grow because of its drought-resisting tap roots.

In moist and fertile soil, it quickly yields a good crop. Late in May or early in June, sowing may be done out of doors, but for early crops indoor sowing in March or April is recommended. Sprouting is slow — 10 to 13 days. Seeds should be sprinkled very lightly and barely covered with earth. Rows must be 15 to 18 in. (38 to 45 cm) apart. Hoeing and weeding are important, especially during the early growing period. Cutting should be done at ground level. Cut only as much as you need from day to day.

Parsley may be dried out for winter storage.

Parsnip

Parsnips need a very rich, deep, and fresh soil.

When properly grown, the roots can attain a diameter of 2.5 in. (6 cm) and a length of 18 in. (45 cm). For good straight rooting, sow in deeply spaded soil.

Sprouting is very slow. Sowing should be done as early as possible in the spring to a depth of only ¼ in. (5 mm). When the plants are 3 to 4 in. (8 to 10 cm) high, the rows should be thinned, leaving 4 to 5 in. (10 to 12 cm) between plants and 18 to 24 in. (45 to 60 cm) between rows.

Wait for the first frost before bringing in any of your parsnips. You will get better, sweeter-tasting vegetables if you leave them in the ground until late in the fall, after the ground begins to freeze.

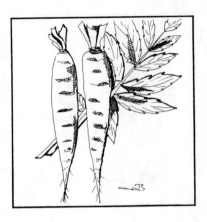

Pimento, mild and strong

Mild pimento is in great demand in Canada. Much sun and well-drained soil are required. Loam is not recommended since this would give you a plant with much foliage but little fruit.

Sow indoors in March. Sprouting takes 15 to 20 days. Replanting must be done in pots or in boxes when plants are about 1 in. (2.5 cm) high. The seedlings are very susceptible to frost, so transplanting into the ground should wait until early in June. Spacing between rows should be 30 to 36 in. (76 to 90 cm) and between plants 15 to 18 in. (38 to 45 cm).

Full maturity is reached in 60 to 80 days. A spicy-tasting variety is grown in Canada: the small red pimento. It is used mostly for ketchup and pickle spicing.

Potato

This vegetable is one of the easiest to grow. You may use bits of peel or potato pieces that have been sliced to obtain sprouts.

A furrow 4 to 6 in. (10 to 15 cm) deep is made and sprouts or pieces of peel are placed in it at intervals of 4 to 6 in. (10 to 15 cm) with a 4 in. (10 cm) soil cover. Planting must be done between early May and June 15 so that you will have ripe potatoes that will keep throughout the next winter. Germination takes from 12 to 18 days and earthing-up (drawing soil up around the plant with a hoe) should be done every 15 days throughout the summer. You may start bringing in small potatoes by August 10. Your crop will be mature between September 15 and November 1 and it must be brought in as soon as it is mature. Spacing between rows should be 24 to 30 in. (60 to 75 cm). During the summer, any insects that appear on the leaves should be removed. Use chemical fertilizer 7-7-7 or 10-10-10, deep in every furrow, on the scale of one handful for every 10 ft. (3 m) of furrow.

Pumpkin

The pumpkin is a children's favourite because of its association with Hallowe'en. Some people used pumpkin for jam or pies, and others clean and roast the seeds.

Pumpkins should be planted as soon as the earth begins to warm up, on hillocks 8 ft. (2.5 m) apart. Thinning must be done so that there will be three plants on each hillock.

Pumpkins are harvested at the end of the summer or early in the fall, at about the time that apples are picked. They should be stored in a cool place.

This vegetable cannot be recommended for small kitchen gardens. In large plantations of pumpkins, the leaves become so dense and thick no weeds can grow.

Radish

Radishes were grown in China more than 3,000 years ago. It is therefore, not surprising that we have a great many varieties today. Radishes may be sown between other slow-growing vegetables. Full maturity takes 25 to 30 days. Spacing between plants should be 1 in. (2.5 cm).

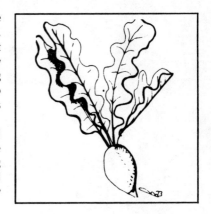

Radishes stand up well to cold weather, and outdoor sowing may be done any time after the beginning of May. A light and rich black soil should be used. Liquid fertilizer may be applied every 15 days.

Cover seeds with about $1/2$ in. (1 cm) of soil and keep them wet; dry weather is very hard on radishes, causing them to become twisted and to run to seed.

For a steady supply of fresh radishes, sow a few seeds regularly every week, from the end of April to September 15.

PICTURES

Page

57 — Border garden

58 — Peonies

59-top — Bellflowers

59-bottom — Spring garden

60 — Shrub and flower border

61 — Annual planting

62 — Hanging basket of petunias and peony border

63-top — Onions

63-bottom — Gourds

64-top — Asparagus

64-bottom — Pole beans

Savory

Of Mediterranean origin, savory is a small perennial shrub with stems 18 to 24 in. (45 to 60 cm) high. Flowering occurs in August and full maturity in September. This plant thrives in different soils and can be grown successfully almost anywhere. Sowing is done in May. Spacing between rows should be 24 in. (60 cm) and between plants 2 to 3 in. (about 5 to 8 cm). Seeds should not be buried deep, and a light watering after seeding should be enough.

When flowering begins, the plant should be picked. Avoid low cutting, since this causes woody stems to appear.

This plant will not tolerate stagnant moisture. Stems should be topped to a height of 4 in. (10 cm) for the winter. The next year, new stems will appear and form new plants.

Spinach

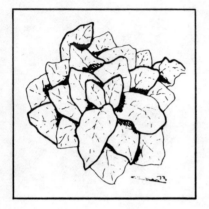

Spinach is easy to grow and it grows rapidly. It thrives especially in fresh, rich soil in a temperate climate.

Sowing is done early in the spring, as soon as the ground can be worked, in rows ½ in. (1 cm) deep. Spacing between plants should be 3 to 4 in. (7 to 10 cm) and between rows 15 in. (38 cm). To harvest crops right up to September 30, seed-beds should be renewed every 15 days. Spinach ripens between 27 and 32 days after sowing. Summer heat may cause the plants to go to seed.

This is a vegetable that requires rotation; unless you practise rotation you are likely to have to cope with diseases.

For the kitchen garden, the New Zealand spinach is recommended. It may be cooked as spinach or eaten raw.

Spring Onion

Spring onions are baby onions obtained from the preceding year's seedlings. These should be planted by the end of May or early in June, very close together and covered with no more than 1/2 in. (1 cm) of soil.

Because they are squeezed together and deprived of moisture and nourishment, the onions do not grow large, although they do reach maturity.

When they are ready, pick them and dry them carefully. The smaller ones may be saved for planting next year.

Spring onions should be grow in rows, like regular onions.

They may be served two or three weeks after planting, or after ripening fully.

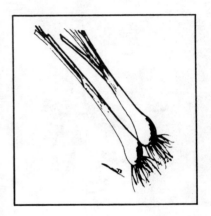

Tomato

The tomato is one of the most widely grown fruits in Canada. It is highly regarded, has many uses, and is very rich in vitamins.

For an early crop, sowing is done in February inside; replanting is done after 20 or 25 days, in preparation for planting outdoors around May 15. Spacing between plants should be 2 or 3 ft. (60 to 90 cm).

For a normal crop, sowing should be done in March or April. Replanting is done into hotbeds, and the seedlings are transplanted into the ground around the end of May. Early-crop tomatoes are picked around mid-July.

The four most popular varieties are:

1. The Red Patio, a very small red tomato, about 1 in. (2.5 cm) in diameter. At maturity, the plant is about 12 in. (30 cm) high. It is a most attractive plant. It is easy to grow in pots, so provides fresh tomatoes all winter.

2. Rather early-maturing, the Beefsteak gives large tomatoes of up to 9 oz. (250 gr.) each. It is a vigorous plant, compact, strong, and highly productive. Its fine dark red tomatoes are preferred by many families.

3. Bonny Best is early-maturing and gives delicious red tomatoes of a fair size.
4. Finally, there is the Pink Glamour, a nice rosy tomato of about 6 in. (15 cm) in diameter.

Barring drought, no watering need be done in a normal summer. When planting, to prevent burning of the roots, fertilizer should be spread around the base of the plant at a distance of 8 in. (20 cm). If a water soluble fertilizer is used, it may be applied directly at the base of the plant.

A sunny plot is important. If mildew gets on your tomatoes, you can fight it with the help of a special powder available at nurseries.

Turnip (rutabaga)

To get good turnips, constant care is required. Do not use the same ground year after year. A four-to-five year rotation is advisable.

Sowing should be done by mid-June, ³/₄ in. (2 cm) deep in rows about 2 ft. (60 cm) apart. There should be 6 in. (15 cm) between the plants. When the plants are 2 or 3 in. (5 or 8 cm) high, the rows should be thinned out. To avoid trouble, do not try to hoe or weed deeper than 1 or 2 in. (2.5 to 5 cm).

Rutabagas take 60 to 100 days to reach maturity. Quality and flavour will be much improved by light frost. For storage of turnips, the temperature should be kept at about 32° F (0° C) and humidity at around 90 per cent.

Watermelon

Water melons are very easily grown in the garden but you need lots of room. If you sow early in June on open, rising ground you will have ripe fruit in September.

On each mound sow seven or eight seeds 1 in. (2.5 cm) deep. When the plants are 3 or 4 in. (8 to 10 cm) high, thin them out keeping only the three or four best ones.

Spacing between mounds should be 6 to 8 ft. (1.8 to 2.4 m). For an early crop, pot-sowing may be done in April.

Open-ground planting should not be done until early in June, since these plants do not stand up well against the cold.

Many varieties are available. Maturity is reached 75 to 95 days after sowing.

Herbs for seasoning

I find the month of September the best time for gathering aromatic herbs and herbs for seasoning. Most of them are then at the peak of their flavour. Flavour comes from different kinds of oil stored in the tissues, so it is important to pick herbs in good time, before the oils have a chance to dry out. If leaves are to be gathered, this should be done just before flowering; if it is seeds that are being collected, they will be ready just before they would fall off and before turning from green to brown. It is easy to lose the oils if your harvesting, drying, and storing are not done under good conditions.

Drying technique

To dry herbs, they should be spread out on lattice-work or wire-netting, or tied into bundles and hung up. This can be done in the attic or in an empty room as long as there is good ventilation and no direct sunlight. For hanging up herbs, you can stretch a rope across a room close to the ceiling. Be sure to keep them out of sunlight, which will discolour your herbs.

I advise against using an oven for drying, because there is a real risk of losing all the cooking value of your herbs. If you are obliged to use an oven, leave the oven door open and keep the temperature low (250° F — 120° C). This is so that the leaves will not fade and the oils will not be lost.

If the normal drying method is used, foliage will be dry and crisp after seven to ten days. Herbs should dry out rather rapidly, and to help this they should be tied in small bundles. When they are dry they should be placed loosely in jars. Whole leaves keep their flavour best. Containers should be sealed and stored in a dark, dry place. Leaves may be crushed before using.

Annual flowers

Their use

Annual flowers enhance the garden and are an inexpensive source of cut flowers for the house. They are also widely used for balcony and window decoration and in borders laid out with perennials they are excellent for filling gaps that occur as earlier flowers fade.

They are also frequently used in front of shrubs whose flowering has finished, in empty spots reserved for growing shrubs, between the kitchen garden and the lawn, and in flower beds.

Annual flowers complete their life cycle in a single year.

Growing

There are two ways of growing annuals: by planting seeds and by purchasing plants. The first is much cheaper. If you are going to use seeds, sow them six to eight weeks before you intend to plant seedlings in the ground. Quality seeds and good soil are necessary.

Sowing should be done in wooden boxes about 2 in. (5 cm) high. Distribute the seeds on a bed of leaf mould and cover them with dry vermiculite. Sprinkle lightly with water. For good results keep the temperature between 65° and 70° F (about 19 to 20° C).

Light is a very important factor. Move your containers into the light as soon as your plants start to come up. Outdoor transplanting should be done on a dull day and into moist soil. For a few days, your young plants should not get too much direct sunlight. Before you plant, hoe and weed the ground thoroughly.

Choosing your flowers

How do you go about choosing varieties that will be well-suited to your needs? One of the best ways is to ask your dealer. Tell him what and where the flowers will be, especially whether they will be in full light, semi-shade, or shade. Also tell him what kind of planting you have in mind. Are your plants for a rock-garden, for borders, to provide cut flowers, or to be displayed indoors? Some varieties are very easy to grow and even thrive in poor soil, or with little light. And the low cost of annuals makes them all the more tempting.

Climbing plants

Among the many kinds of annuals are some that climb — and these are useful for covering a fence, a trellis, a wall, or the side of a veranda.

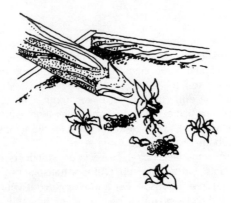

To transplant tiny seedlings prick them out of the seedbed very carefully with a notched stick or a pencil.

Ageratum

This is the perfect plant for rock-gardens, for edging, or for window boxes and planters. It is stocky, compact, and decorative, and its flowers are blue or rose in colour, depending on the variety you select.

Seeds take 12 or 15 days to sprout and plants flower all summer, starting about two months after sowing, which is generally done indoors, in March or April.

Plants grow 6 to 9 in. (15 to 23 cm) high and are ball-shaped.

This plant is strong, but it cannot stand a hot dry location.

Ageratum thrive in half-shade. Keep plants well watered, and cut off dead flowers immediately.

Alyssum

Alyssum is a wonderful asset to any rock-garden. Dwarf and stocky, it stays in bloom all summer and keeps flowering until frost. Its flowers are sweet-smelling, and, according to the variety, white, blue, pink, or yellow. They are used for edging or for window boxes.

The flowers come out 55 to 75 days after sowing. Germination takes five to seven days. Seeds may be planted out of doors, but if they are planted inside, in April, the flowers will appear much earlier and they will be bonnier. Transplanting is done in May or June.

Amaranth

The amaranth is a beautiful, decorative plant with multi-coloured foliage. It may be used as a background for borders or in clumps. Seeds may be sown indoors in March or directly into the ground in May. Sprouting is slow (12 to 14 days) and flowering occurs 75 to 90 days after sowing. The little flowers are displayed in long, hanging clusters. The height is 30 to 36 in. (75 to 90 cm).

Three varieties are available. The Caudatus (Foxtail) is a tall plant with hanging red flowers and velvety foliage. The Rising Sun Aurora has scarlet-purple foliage, richly speckled with yellow, bronze, or green; height 20 to 24 in. (50 to 60 cm). Early Splendor grows 4 to 5 ft. (1.2 to 1.5 m) tall and is greatly admired for its wine-red foliage in the lower part and bright scarlet foliage at the top. Spacing between plants should be 18 to 24 in. (45 to 60 cm). At the end of September, plants should be potted and brought back indoors.

Bellflower

Campanula

This plant is ideal for borders and rock-gardens. It produces, in profusion, beautiful bell-shaped flowers.

Flowers do not emerge until six months after sowing, so seeds should be planted indoors early in February. The height ranges from 1 to 2 ft. (30 to 60 cm), depending on the variety.

This plant is often used to fill base spots in rock-gardens. Heavy flowering starts in August, as long as early sowing was done indoors, and continues until October.

Many varieties are available and colours range from blue to intense violet.

Campanula carpatica which has open clear blue or white flowers and *Campanula glomerata* are two varieties that are easy to find in Canada.

Calendula

The calendula is often called the pot marigold. Height varies from 15 to 18 in. (38 to 45 cm) and they are rugged and easy to grow. Indoor sowing in March or April and outdoor transplanting by the end of May is the general rule. Spacing between plants should be 12 to 15 in. (30 to 38 cm). Germination takes 10 to 12 days. The plants will continue to bloom until November.

Earlier planting generally gives larger flowers. Flowers should be cut as soon as they start to fade.

Many varieties are available, among them the Pacific Beauty Mixture, which has beautiful colouring, the Orange Pacific Beauty, with full double flowers, and the Yellow and Cream Pacific Beauty. The entire Pacific Beauty strain has been bred to withstand summer heat.

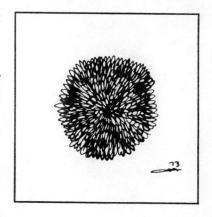

Carnation

The Carnation belongs to a large family with a great many varieties. It is used for borders, round beds, clumps, flower pots, and window-boxes.

The stems are thick and the main one usually grows to a height of 18 to 24 in. (45 to 60 cm). Colouring depends on the variety.

It takes several months to get flowers from seeds. Sow indoors in March and you will have beautiful blossoms from mid-summer until early frost.

In the fall, select the nicest plants and pot them, after cutting them back. After a while, they will flower again.

With their sweet clover smell, carnations are very popular. All sizes from dwarf to giant are available. Some are better suited than others to outdoor growing. Consult your dealer.

Celosia (cockscomb)

There are two forms of this old-fashioned plant: the cockscomb celosia, which really does look like a cockscomb, and the plumosa variety, whose flowers are like ostrich feathers. The feathered cockscomb, with flowers in a pyramidal shaped plume, is illustrated here.

Popular on account of its beauty and fine colouring, this plant is easy to grow. It creates a marvellous effect when used for strips or borders. Indoor sowing should be done in March, and plants should be put out in early June in a very rich soil. Full exposure to the sun is necessary.

Cut flowers may be dried in the shade to be used as everlasting flowers.

Some varieties are dwarf and some are giant. The giant celosia can reach a height of 2 or 3 ft. (60 to 90 cm) and its very bright flowers have red or orange colouring.

The dwarf grows no higher than 12 in. (30 cm) and it flowers are red, yellow, and other colours.

Centaurea (Bachelor's button)

This hardy annual also called the cornflower or ragged robin is one of the easiest of all plants to grow.

Outdoor planting may be done in early May, with spacing of 8 to 10 in. (20 to 25 cm). Flowering continues all summer. This plant is mostly used in clumps and for edge decoration.

Germination takes 10 to 15 days. Flowering occurs 55 to 60 days after sowing. The plants are generally 10 to 24 in. (25 to 60 cm) high. The plant can easily be propagated and all specimens have identical shaping. For the slow-flowering varieties, indoor sowing should start in March.

The flowers are thistle-like in appearance. Cut flowers keep in water for 10 to 12 days.

China-aster

The china aster, an annual, is available in three sizes; the 8 to 12 in. (20 to 30 cm) dwarf; the 15 to 24 in. (38 to 60 cm) medium-sized; and the up to 34 in. (85 cm) for the large size.

Plant seeds indoors at the end of March or early in April for transplanting in June and flowering by mid-July.

Dwarf varieties may be placed in the front of borders, while the taller variety are best at the back of your garden, or for filling corners. Taller plants should be pinched back several times in late spring and early summer so that they'll be bushier.

Plant asters in a sunny place with a spacing of 15 to 18 in. (38 to 45 cm) between plants. Many colours are available: blue, pink, white, violet, red. Some varieties have many-coloured plants and even of divided colours, as with the super-giant aster, rising to 3 ft. (90 cm) and giving beautiful cut flowers.

The Coloured Carpet is a popular dwarf variety. It has many colours and grows no higher than 8 in. (20 cm).

In the medium size, there is the Perfection aster with multi-coloured flowers. It grows to 30 in. (75 cm) and has stiff stems and a double flower with a 4 in. (10 cm) diameter.

All china asters are excellent as cut flowers.

Cineraria

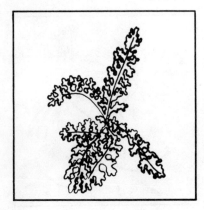

This plant is not known for its flowers so much as for its silvery foliage, which is often used for contrast with greens and with multicoloured flowers. It also may be displayed in hanging baskets, and is first rate around shrubs or for edging.

Indoor sowing should be done in March or April, followed by transplanting outdoors at the end of May. Plants should be spaced from 8 to 10 in. (20 to 25 cm) apart.

As the flower is of little consequence, the shoots with floral buds should be pinched off.

The cineraria is very sensitive to moisture and cannot tolerate cold weather.

Propagation is done with cuttings.

Cosmos

This easy-to-grow plant keeps on flowering until late in the fall. Its delicate foliage is highly decorative. The large graceful flowers are white or pink and 4 to 5 in. (10 to 13 cm) in diameter.

Cosmos do well in the shade as well as in the sun and are mainly used as backgrounds for shrub borders or for moss plantings. They are also a good source of cut flowers.

Plant seeds in the ground in May and you will have flowers from August to October. For earlier results, indoor sowing should be done in April. Sprouting takes eight to ten days.

Plants are generally 18 to 36 in. (45 to 90 cm) high. Flowering will start 12 to 13 weeks after sowing.

Dahlia

For a number of years, dahlias of the double-flower variety seemed to be the popular ones. Nowadays, single dahlias occupy the first place in public favour. Both types, however, are ideal for mass plantings in clumps because of their beautiful showy colouring.

Indoor sowing of seeds should be done in March, followed by pot replanting. Outdoor planting should be done in June. Spacing between plants should be 15 to 24 in. (38 to 60 cm). Dahlias give flowers prolifically from July to October. Tending them is not difficult but make sure the soil around them does not dry. A mulch will help.

After the first frost, plants must be brought inside. During the winter, tubers should be kept in a cool cellar.

In April of the next year plant the tubers in pots of 7 to 8 in. (18 to 20 cm) in diameter, for flowering in July.

Cut dahlias last best when picked in the late afternoon or early morning. Keep them in a dark cool place for an hour or so before putting them in an arrangement.

Gilliflower

This is one of our finest annual plants, remarkable for the variety and colouring of its flowers. Some varieties also have an exquisite fragrance. This plant is ideal for edges and clumps, as well as for borders, and it also provides beautiful cut flowers.

For an early crop, sow indoors in March or April and put out when the soil warms. Blossoms will appear seven to ten weeks after sowing. Between 10 and 12 days are required for sprouting. Many varieties are available and heights range from 12 to 30 in. (30 to 75 cm).

This is a first-class plant for your garden.

Everlasting (Honesty)

Lunaria annua

Although most attractive in the garden, everlasting *Lunaria annua* are mainly grown for drying. To get flowers for drying, cut off stems when the buds are beginning to open out and the blossoms are beginning to take shape. Remove any leaves, and hang the flowers upside down in a dark, dry place for two or three weeks. Once dried, the flowers will keep for a considerable time.

Light soil and full exposure to the sun are recommended. Indoor sowing should be done in April and outdoor planting early in June. Germination takes six to nine days.

If you decide to leave the plants in the garden, you will have flowers from July until the first frost.

Flowers are of varying shapes and sizes from daisy-like to little cat-tails to a ball form. Another common type is the strawflower.

Morning glory (Bindweed)

Convolvulus

Bindweed or morning glory, a climbing plant, was one seen on nearly every fence. It is easy to look after and grows rapidly. The trumpet-like flowers in blue, rose, red or white stay open most of the day in cloudy weather — in bright sunlight they wilt.

A light, warm soil is required. Sow the seeds as soon as the earth has warmed up. Stem length is from $1^1/_2$ to 10 ft. (.45 to 3 m), according to the variety. I suggest that you buy one of the dwarf varieties for flower stands. These are highly decorative and are a welcome change from the too-common petunia.

Transplanting is often unsuccessful, so plant seeds in pots, which should have three plants each, after thinning. It will take the plants 75 to 90 days to flower.

Nasturtium

The nasturtium is perfect for borders, clumps, hanging baskets, and flower-boxes. The warm, bright colouring of the flowers is a fine contrast with the foliage. This beautiful climbing plant grows easily in almost any kind of soil, but prefers a thin light soil, and a warm, airy place.

Outdoor sowing should wait until the end of May or early in June. Spacing between plants should be 12 to 18 in. (30 to 45 cm). For early flowering, try doing your outdoor sowing by the end of April.

Many varieties are available. The dwarf ones grow approximately 12 in. (30 cm) high; the semi-climbing ones about 3 ft. (90 cm) high; and the giant climbing varieties, given warm weather, will spread over trellises and lattice-work very rapidly.

The nasturtium often becomes insect-infested in summer. Talk to your nursery about a suitable spray. Never fertilize this plant or you'll get all leaves and no flowers.

Petunia (Saint Joseph)

The petunia is also known in Canada by the name of Saint Joseph and is probably found in more borders, rock-gardens, clumps, flower-boxes and hanging baskets than any other annual. It is popular partly because it is so easy to grow. It is also a plant that suits our climate perfectly.

The petunia does best in the sun but it also gets along quite well in the shade. Flowering is continuous from spring to fall. Seeds should be sown indoors in March and pressed firmly into the soil. To retain moisture, use a plastic cover at the start, but remove it when sprouting occurs, after 10 or 15 days. Water at the base. Plants are sturdy when they have reached a height of 2 or 3 in. (5 to 8 cm).

When the seedlings are 1 in. (2.5 cm) high, transplant them into boxes with 2 in. (5 cm) spacing. Put out about May.

You can get petunias in many different colours, and there is a double variety with carnation-like flowers. Petunias generally should be cut back in mid-summer so they become bushier. You should feed them after cutting back.

Snapdragon

This plant is grown in nearly every part of Canada. All varieties give abundant flowers, in a variety of colours. Plants may be laid out in bunches or amongst other flowers as accent spots.

Indoor sowing should be done in February or March for planting outdoors late in May or early in June. After planting seeds, keep the temperature between 65° and 75° (19° and 22° C). Germination is slow — 15 to 18 days.

To get strong, stocky plants, cut them back severely at least twice each summer. This plant thrives in all kinds of soil, in full sun or in the shade, and with no special care.

If you plant seeds indoors, you will have flowers in the garden in July and they will last until early frost.

Several sizes are available, from giant to dwarf. The height varies from 8 to 24 in. (20 to 60 cm). For rockgardens, dwarf varieties are recommended.

Sweet pea

Sweet peas are highly favoured by gardeners in Canada and many people grow them just to be cut — even a handful of flowers casually placed in a small vase is delightful.

Prepare for planting early in the fall, by digging the soil to a depth of 12 to 18 in. (30 to 45 cm), mixing in plenty of fertilizer. Plant seeds very early in the spring at 6 in. (15 cm) intervals in a furrow 6 in. (15 cm) deep and cover them with 2 in. (5 cm) of soil. The furrows should be filled in gradually as the seedlings grow.

This plant needs lots of sun and very moist soil. Fertilizer should be applied every 15 days. Sweet peas need to be supported by wires, a trellis, a fence, or a wall.

The foliage should never be watered but the roots must always have moisture. In dry weather, the plants must be given a lot of attention. Keep cutting off the flowers to encourage more blooms.

Perennial plants

Borders

Border gardens with perennials have irresistible appeal. In the early spring-time, you can watch the plants rise out of the ground with all their happy memories. With proper planning, you will be able to get flowers from early in the spring to the end of the fall.

Locations

A border should, as a rule, be placed in front of a green background, such as a hedge or shrubs. It will look better that way. To allow the perennials to spread, the spacing between plants should be 3 to 4 ft. (90 to 120 cm). a sunny and well-drained spot is preferable for this kind of border.

Preparation

The ground must be well prepared. This means removing the surface layer of about 6 in. (15 cm) and thoroughly digging up the sub-soil. The surface soil should be mixed with fertilizer before it is replaced. All of this should be done in the fall.

Layout

Draw a diagram to scale that shows where you are going to put your plants. It is essential to have a general idea of the performance, flowering dates, and colouring of the varieties you intend to plant. During the first flowering season, note down any changes you think you should make. Remember to take into consideration how much time you are willing to devote to your garden. Don't put in more plants than you will enjoy maintaining.

Care and upkeep

Once the border is well established, you must take steps to keep weeds in check. Weekly hoeing and weeding are necessary. As soon as the flowers have faded, remove them, unless you need seeds in which case you will leave them on the plant until the petals drop. Remove dry foliage as well.

Rather drastic topping should be done in the fall.

In the springtime, it is important to examine the roots. If they are uncovered, earthing up must be done to prevent the sun from drying them out.

Borders should be fertilized every year. As soon as the frost is gone, hoeing and weeding should start. If the weather is dry, do a generous watering once a week; this must be a deep watering since a light one would bring the roots to the surface, exposing them to the heat of the sun.

Transplanting

At almost any time, many perennials may be transplanted from one place to another. For plants that blossom before June 15, transplant early in September. For late-flowering plants, transplant in May. It is always wise to consult an experienced gardener or your nursery as to the best procedure for transplanting this or that variety.

Chrysanthemum

More and more varieties of chrysanthemum are becoming available from year to year. The new ones are much more cold-resistant and the colouring is more varied.

Propagation may be carried out either by division, cutting a branch off an old plant and rooting it, or by planting seeds. Sprouting takes 10 to 18 days. "Mums" are easy to grow and bloom 75 to 110 days after indoor seeding, depending on the variety. If you sow seeds indoors in March and set them out when the ground warms, you will have continuous flowering until the first frost. Spacing between plants should be 15 to 18 in. (38 to 45 cm). Some varieties of chrysanthemum are considered to be perennials. Consult your dealer about this when you are ordering.

Dwarf varieties generally grow about 12 in. (30 cm) high and the giant ones grow to 4 ft. (1.20 m). Between these two extremes, you may obtain chrysanthemums of many sizes.

After hard frost in the fall cut your "mums" back to about 5 in. (13 cm) and put a mulch over them to keep the roots from being heaved up by the frost.

Geranium

This plant plays a very important decorative role in our gardens, because of the beautiful, strong colouring of its foliage and flowers. Its hardiness also contributes greatly to its popularity in Canada.

Plants may be obtained by seeding, but the usual method is through cuttings. When the best blossoming season is over, plants should be cut back by two-thirds and the best stems kept for propagation. Cut off 5 in. (13 cm) sections and strip off leaves. The stems should be dipped in a solution containing hormones before being planted in a deep box of moist black soil mixed with sand and "stimulite". The box should be covered with plastic to keep the moisture constant and to promote rooting. Once the rooting is complete, replant the plants in pots in preparation for safe planting later, in the garden.

In the fall, around October 15, bring plants in and repot them in pots 6 to 8 in. (15 to 20 cm) in diameter. Put the plants in a sunny place and water them twice a week. If you have a cold cellar you can keep all your plants there in pots 6 to 8 in. (15 to 20 cm) deep, watering them every second week. Use them in March as cuttings.

Geraniums bloom better when slightly rootbound and prefer good soakings rather than frequent sprinklings of water.

Larkspur

Larkspur used to be seen in every garden, it was so popular. Nowadays, unfortunately, it is not so common.

This perennial is remarkable for its erect bearing, for its finely ribboned foliage, and for its close flower clusters. The height varies considerably between the different varieties.

Transplanting is rarely successful; sowing in the ground should be done in May. Broadcast the seeds and thin the plants later to 8-9 in. (20 cm) apart. Germination takes 15 to 20 days. Larkspur will remain in bloom from the end of July until the first frost. It needs a good garden soil, and a place that is sunny for a good part of the day.

On the average, fully-grown plants are 3 to 5 ft. (.90 to 1.5 m) high. This perennial should be planted at the back of your garden.

Pansy

This plant is sometimes an annual and sometimes a biennial or perennial, depending on the conditions and the ground in which it is grown.

Indoor seeding is done in February or March. Germination takes 10 to 12 days. The small plants are transplanted in boxes and finally put into the garden early in June. For continuous blooming, flowers should be cut as soon as they begin to fade. This prevents seeds from forming instead of new flowers, which will continue to appear until the first frost.

Many varieties are available.

The plants should be left in the ground for the winter. If they are on high ground there will be no problem. Try to prevent damage to the plants by ice. In the spring, you should have fine plants and beautiful flowers from early May until the end of the summer. These plants do not grow very high — 6 to 8 in. (15 to 20 cm). Spacing should be 10 to 12 in. (25 to 30 cm).

Peony

Peonies should be planted between September 5 and 20. Obtain some 3- to-5-year-old plants and separate them into two or three clumps, each containing a minimum of three to five rhizomes. Plant them in a sunny place, close to any large trees.

For each plant, prepare a hole 12 in. (30 cm) deep and 18 in. (45 cm) in diameter, filled with good rich topsoil. The rhizomes should be placed in the soil at a depth of 3 to 5 in. (8 to 12 cm). Many people fail to follow this rule, and then complain about the lack of flowers in the first year. The plants should be protected with 4 in. (10 cm) of mulch (straw or leaves). Branches placed over the bed will help snow to collect on top of the mulch. Flowering generally occurs in the first year, although sometimes, if the rhizomes are small, flowers will not appear until the second year.

On one of the first fine days of spring, remove the branches. Peony shoots start to come out of the ground very early, and budding will begin in June. By the end of June or early July, you will have a fine display of colourful blossoms spreading a delicate scent through your garden.

Around the end of October cut off stems 1 or 2 in. (2.5 to 5 cm) above the ground.

Windows, Balcony gardens

How many apartment dwellers complain that they cannot get out into the country to enjoy the open air, the trees and the flowers! With a little imagination, a few cents, and a love for plants, wonders can be performed right at home. Here are some ways to put more colour and a little perfume into your daily life.

Care

Flowers in a window or on a balcony, will not grow by themselves. They need food and protection from street dust and dirt and when the weather is warm and very dry, or the sunshine is strong, frequent attention is required. Before starting a window or balcony decoration, check with your landlord concerning municipal bylaws. The owner of the building should be consulted as to the kind of installation that you can place on your window or balcony. You should then take into account the weight of the container and the heavy wet soil. Everything must be held firmly in place, because you could be held responsible in case of an accident.

Containers

Your plant dealer can supply containers in various shapes and sizes. Some are made of wood, some of stone, plastic, metal, clay or earthenware. Remember that your containers should be at least 8 in. (20 cm) deep, otherwise your plants will die from lack of water. Pots should be placed in pot stands that can be fastened to lattice-work, balcony railings, a window sill, or in hanging baskets. Wooden, metal, or plastic boxes should be used for small shrubs or climbing plants.

Colour

When you select your flower containers, choose colours that will blend harmoniously and that will match the building. It would not be appropriate, for instance, to have window-shutters in one colour and flower boxes in another.

Drainage and filling

When preparing your pots and containers, good drainage must always be considered. This is why a bottom opening is essential, even though you cover it with a layer of small stones, vermiculite, or other material. First, add a layer of at least 2 in. (5 cm) of chards, crock or stones to provide drain protection. Then pour in the potting medium to within about 1 or 1¹/₂ in. (3-4 cm) from the top. At the top of the conainer, put an additional moss layer to retain surface moisture. Soil must always be moist but not sticky and *never* dry. It should be porous but, because of this, moisture is easily lost. This is why regular watering is necessary. Soil should be changed every year.

Planting

When planting, remember that plants need space to grow. For dwarf varieties, spacing should be between 4 and 6 in. (10 and 15 cm); for medium sized plants, 6 to 8 in. (15 to 20 cm) are required, and for taller and larger

ones, 8 to 10 in. (20 to 25 cm) must be allowed. Two parallel rows may be made in window boxes when planting. Then the plants will grow in a rectangular pattern.

A few examples

With an 8 in. (20 cm) wide container, a single centre row should be planted for average size plants; for dwarf plants, two parallel rows are possible. With a 10 to 12 in. (25 to 30 cm) wide container, three rows may be planted: at the front, you might use plants with trailing leaves; in the centre, a row of medium size plants. Taller specimens may be set in the third row. This third row should be up against a wall, or balcony railing for support.

Balcony vegetables

Vegetable growing on a balcony won't save you money but it is fun and gives you the chance to get occasional fresh vegetables for the table. Vegetables respond well to this kind of environment. Half a day of sunlight is required regularly. Start with tomatoes. Put a single plant in a large pot and prop it as it grows. Flowers may be planted at the plant's base.

Climbing plants

These plants can transform ugly walls into beautifully flowered areas or they may be used to give a measure of privacy. Containers should have firm brackets.

Vertical flower stands and hanging baskets

Vertical flower stands come in a variety of shapes. They may hang on a wall or may be in the form of a standing rack. Long-stem moss should be used as an outer protection for the plants roots. Un-pot the plant and wrap the roots by placing moss around the earth. Planting should be deeper and firmer than in flower stands. Using a can with a long spout, water the moss well. Soluble fertilizer should be applied once a week. The moss must never be allowed to dry out.

A hanging basket is another alternative. As if you were building a nest, line the inside of the basket completely with moss. Plants must then be set in place with small amounts of soil and some moss between each one of them. Once the basket is planted, immerse it in water until it is soaked. The same attention is required as for vertical stands. For best results, choose some plants with trailing foliage.

SEED CALENDAR FOR GARDEN FLOWERS

January	February	March	April	May	June
					PERENNIAL
cineraria	ageratum	ageratum	alyssum	centaurea	bellflower
gloxinia	bellflower	amaranth	calendula	cosmos	chrysanthemum
pansy	carnation	calendula	cineraria	larkspur	clematis
	pansy	carnation	petunia	morning glory	columbine
	snap-dragon	celosia		nasturtium	daisy
		chrysanthemum		sweet pea	delphinium
		cineraria		zinnia	digitalis
		dahlia			hollyhock
		gilliflower			narcissus
		petunia			poppy
		snap-dragon			primrose
					viola

July	August	September	October	November	December
PERENNIAL					
pansy	african violet	african violet	african violet	african violet	geranium
	cactus	cactus	cactus	cactus	tuberous
	gloxinia	cineraria			begonia

VEGETABLE SEED CALENDAR FOR KITCHEN GARDENS

January	February	March	April	May	June
	INDOORS	INDOORS	INDOORS	OUTDOORS	OUTDOORS
	artichoke	artichoke	basil	basil	beans
	egg plant	asparagus	brussels sprouts	beet	beet
		broccoli	chinese cabbage	carrot	carrot
		cabbage	chives	chicory	corn
		cauliflower	melon	corn	cress
		celery	potato	dill	cucumber
		egg-plant	radish	endive	dill
		lettuce		endive	radish
		melon cantaloupe		(broad leaved)	spinach
		onion		fennel	turnip-rutabaga
		parsley		garlic	watermelon
		pimento		gourd	
		tomato		leek	
				lettuce	
				parsley	
				parsnip	
				pumpkin	
				radish	
				savory	
				spinach	
				spring onion	

VEGETABLE SEED CALENDAR FOR KITCHEN GARDENS

July	August	September	October	November	December
OUTDOORS					
bean	radish	chervil			
beet	spinach				
carrot					
parsnip					
potato					
radish					
spinach					

ANNUAL CALENDAR

VEGETABLE	DATE SEED	IN	OUT	TRANS-PLAN-TATION	LOCATION		SEED-DEPTH	NUMBER OF DAYS TO MATURITY
					ROWS	PLANTS		
Artichoke	Feb.-March	x		June	48 in. (1.20 m)	12 in. (30 cm)		after the third year
Asparagus	March	x		May	12 in. (30 cm)	4 to 5 ft. (1.20-1.50 m)	1 in. (2.5 cm)	
Basil	April	x	x-May		20 in. (50 cm)	5 to 6 in. (13-15 cm)		65 to 75
Bean	June		x		20 to 24 in. (50-61 cm)		2 in. (5 cm)	52 to 70
Beet	May-June 15		x		12-18 in. (30-46 cm)	2 in. (5 cm)	1/2 in. (1.25 cm)	55 to 70
Broccoli	March	x		end May	3 ft. (91 cm)	15 to 24 in. (37-61 cm)	1/4 in. (.75 cm)	60 to 70
Brussels sprouts	April 20	x			32 in. (80 cm)	20 in. (51 cm)	1/4 in. (.75 cm)	90 to 95
Cabbage	March 20	x		early June	2 ft. (61 cm)	18 in. (46 cm)	1/4 in. (.75 cm)	60 to 75
Carrot	May-June		x		12 in. (30 cm)	1 to 3 in. (2.5-7.5 cm)		65 to 80
Cauliflower	March	x		May	24 to 26 in. (61-66 cm)	18 to 20 in. (46-51 cm)	1/4 in. (.75 cm)	50 to 65
Celery	March	x			2 ft. (61 cm)	9 to 10 in. (23-25 cm)	1/8 in. (.325 cm)	95 to 105
Chervil	May-Aug.		x		15 to 18 in. (38-46 cm)			
Chicory	May		x		18 in. (46 cm)	12 in. (30 cm)	1/4 in. (.75 cm)	95
Chinese Cabbage	April	x		May	2 ft. (61 cm)	10 in. (25 cm)	1/4 in. (.75 cm)	65 to 75
Chives	April	x			all directions			all months
Corn	end May		x		all directions	12 in. (30 cm)	1 in. (2.5 cm)	70 to 100
Cress	June		x		10 or 12 in. (25-30 cm)	4 in. (10 cm)	surface	6 to 8 weeks
Cucumber	June		x		5 ft. (1.50 m)	3 or 4 plants all directions		
Dill	May-June		x		24 in. (61 cm)	3 to 4 in. (7-10 cm)	surface	80 to 86

Egg Plant	Feb.-March	x		June	2 to 3 ft. (61-91 cm)	2 to 3 ft. (61-91 cm)		70 to 75
Endive	May		x		18 in. (46 cm)	5 to 6 in. (13-15 cm)	deep soil	45 to 60
Endive, Broad-leaf	end May		x		18 to 24 in. (46-61 cm)	12 in. (30 cm)		85 to 90
Fennel	May		x		24 to 30 in. (61-76 cm)	5 to 6 in. (13-15 cm)		60 to 75
Garlic	May		x		18 in. (46 cm)	4 in. (10 cm)	surface	85 to 94
Gourd	May		x		4 to 10 ft. (1.20-3 m)	3 plants		52 (summer) 110 (winter)
Laurel								
Leek	May		x		24 to 26 in. (61-65 cm)	4 to 6 in. (10-15 cm)	1/4 in. (.75 cm)	100 to 115
Lettuce	March-April	x	May-June	May	15 to 18 in. (38-46 cm)	15 in. (38 cm)	1/4 in. (.75 cm)	50 to 75
Melon-Cantaloupe	March-April	x		June	4 to 5 ft. (1.20-1.50 m)	3 plants		75 to 90
Mushroom								
Onion	March	x	x-May		15 to 18 in. (38-46 cm)	2 to 3 in. (5-8 cm)		45 to 80
Parsley	May	x-March	x	May	15 to 18 in. (38-46 cm)		surface	60 to 90
Parsnip	May	x	x		18 to 24 in. (46-61 cm)	4 to 5 in. (10-12 cm)	1/4 in. (.75 cm)	60 to 75
Pimento-mild-strong	March	x		June	30 to 36 in. (76-90 cm)	15 to 18 in. (38-46 cm)		70
Potato	March	x		April	28 in. (70 cm)	10 in. (25 cm)		65 to 90
Pumpkin	May		x		8 ft. (2.40 m)	3 plants		75 to 90
Radish	May		x			1 in. (2.5 cm)	1/2 in. (1.25 cm)	20 to 25
Savory	May		x		24 in. (61 cm)	2 to 3 in. (5-8 cm)	surface	
Spinach	May		x		15 in. (38 cm)	3 to 4 in. (7-10 cm)	1/2 in. (1.25 cm)	27 to 32
Spring onion	May		x			very tight	1/2 in. (1.25 cm)	40 to 50
Tomato	February	x		June	2 to 3 ft. (61-91 cm)	18 to 24 in. (45-61 cm)		80 to 130
Turnip-Rutabaga	mid-June		x		2 ft. (61 cm)	6 in. (15 cm)	1/2 to 3/4 in. (1.25-2 cm)	60 to 100
Watermelon	June		x		6 to 8 ft. (1.80-2.40 m)	3 or 4 plants	1 in. (2.5 cm)	75 to 95

Maintenance

Watering: it is difficult to set down exact rules. It is better to water regularly than to wait for leaves to fade. Watering should always be generous.

Fertilizing: plants in pots definitely need food. Fertilize the soil with soluble fertilizer. Never give fertilizer to a dry plant, but give only plain water first, then fertilize the next day.

Insects and disease: insects must be destroyed and diseases controlled as soon as they are spotted. Because they are grouped so close together, balcony and window plants are more exposed to spreading infection than are plants in a garden.

Cleaning: spraying to get rid of street dust should be done at least every other day.

Faded flowers and weeds: these should be removed since they sap energy from plants.

Hoeing: the idea is to break up the surface of the soil allowing heat and water to penetrate more deeply and to destroy weeds.

Spading: turn soil over to loosen its texture prior to planting.

Earthing-up: this task involves moving soil around the plant's stalks and is important for certain vegetables.